Ecosystems
Coral Reefs

Simon Rose

www.av2books.com

AV² provides enriched content that supplements and complements this book. Weigl's AV² books strive to create inspired learning and engage young minds in a total learning experience.

Your AV² Media Enhanced books come alive with...

Audio
Listen to sections of the book read aloud.

Key Words
Study vocabulary, and complete a matching word activity.

Video
Watch informative video clips.

Quizzes
Test your knowledge.

Embedded Weblinks
Gain additional information for research.

Slide Show
View images and captions, and prepare a presentation.

Try This!
Complete activities and hands-on experiments.

... and much, much more!

Go to **www.av2books.com**, and enter this book's unique code.

BOOK CODE

K851263

AV² by Weigl brings you media enhanced books that support active learning.

Published by AV² by Weigl
350 5th Avenue, 59th Floor
New York, NY 10118
Website: www.av2books.com   www.weigl.com

Library of Congress Cataloging-in-Publication Data
Rose, Simon, 1961-
  Coral reefs / Simon Rose.
    pages cm. -- (Ecosystems)
  Includes index.
  ISBN 978-1-62127-484-1 (hardcover : alk. paper) -- ISBN 978-1-62127-487-2 (softcover : alk. paper)
  1. Coral reef ecology--Juvenile literature. 2. Coral reef biology--Juvenile literature. 3. Coral reefs and islands--Juvenile literature. I. Title.
  QH541.5.C7R67 2013
  577.7'89--dc23
                          2012045104

Printed in the United States of America in North Mankato, Minnesota
1 2 3 4 5 6 7 8 9 0 17 16 15 14 13

042013
WEP300113

Project Coordinator Aaron Carr
Design Mandy Christiansen

Every reasonable effort has been made to trace ownership and to obtain permission to reprint copyright material. The publishers would be pleased to have any errors or omissions brought to their attention so that they may be corrected in subsequent printings.

Photo Credits
Weigl acknowledges Getty Images as its primary photo supplier for this title.

Contents

What is a Coral Reef Ecosystem?

Coral reef ecosystems are very fragile. Small changes can affect them greatly.

Earth is home to millions of different **organisms**, all of which have unique living requirements. Organisms interact with the environment they live in, as well as with the other organisms in that environment. These interactions between organisms and their environment create **ecosystems**.

Coral reefs are a type of ecosystem. They are underwater structures made up of colonies of tiny organisms called **coral polyps**. Reef-building coral polyps grow into many different shapes. When these coral polyps die, they leave behind limestone remains. New polyps then grow on these remains. Over years, this cycle increases the size of the coral reef.

Although the total area covered by coral reefs is less than 0.015 percent of Earth's oceans, coral reefs are home to about one quarter of the planet's marine life. Coral reefs are mostly found in shallow, clear, **tropical** waters. Some types of coral exist in cold, deep waters.

Eco Facts

Coral reefs are home to a wide variety of marine organisms, including plants, fish, and reptiles. Coral reefs are among the most diverse ecosystems on Earth.

Levels of Organization in Coral Reef Ecosystems

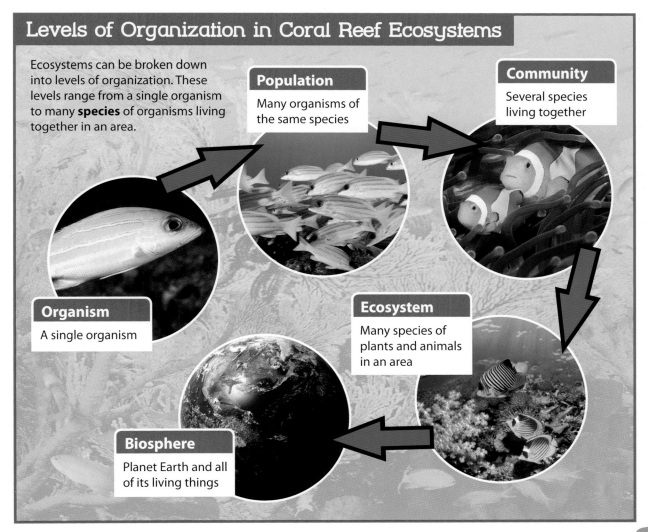

Ecosystems can be broken down into levels of organization. These levels range from a single organism to many **species** of organisms living together in an area.

Population
Many organisms of the same species

Community
Several species living together

Organism
A single organism

Ecosystem
Many species of plants and animals in an area

Biosphere
Planet Earth and all of its living things

Where in the World?

The Great Barrier Reef is made up of more than 900 islands and 3,000 individual coral reefs.

Corals can exist in tropical, **temperate**, and even cold waters. Shallow-water coral reefs are only found in warm waters, relatively close to the **equator**. Most shallow-water reefs are located in the Indian Ocean, the Red Sea, Southeast Asia, and the Pacific Ocean, including the waters around Australia. The world's largest coral reef system is the Great Barrier Reef. It stretches for 1,250 miles (2,012 kilometers) along the coast of Queensland in northeastern Australia.

Pacific Ocean

Also in the Pacific Ocean is the New Caledonia Barrier Reef system. This reef system is 930 miles (1,497 km) long. It surrounds many islands, including New Caledonia's largest island, Grande-Terre.

The Raja Ampat islands comprise the largest marine national park in Indonesia. This reef ecosystem is home to 1,430 species of fish and 603 types of coral.

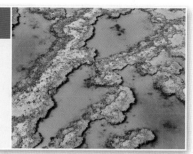

Eco Facts

The Great Barrier Reef is one of the largest structures on Earth. It is large enough to be seen from space.

Indian Ocean

The Republic of Maldives is an island country in the Indian Ocean. It contains around 1,200 reefs and coral islands. The capital city, Male, is built on a coral island. Coral is mined in the Maldives for use in housing. Coral mining harms the reef because the living corals are broken from the reef. The damaged reef can take years to recover.

Red Sea

The Red Sea is part of the Indian Ocean. The Red Sea has some of the most diverse coral reef ecosystems in the world. In the northern part of the Red Sea, reefs are located on steep slopes. In the south, most reefs are located in the shallow waters of the **continental shelf** and around offshore islands.

Caribbean Sea

The Mesoamerican Reef stretches for more than 620 miles (998 km) off the southeastern coast of Mexico. It is the largest barrier reef in the western **hemisphere**. The Andros Barrier Reef in the Bahamas is more than 142 miles (229 km) long. This reef is located near the edge of a very deep trench in the ocean. This trench is called the Tongue of the Ocean. In some places, it is more than 6,000 feet (1,829 meters) deep. At shallower depths, the steep slopes of this trench provide habitats for many reef organisms.

The Andros Barrier Reef is the third longest barrier reef in the world.

Mapping Coral Reefs

This map shows where some of the world's coral reefs are located. Find the place where you live on the map. Do you live close to a coral reef? If not, which coral reef is closest to you?

Red Sea

Location: Red Sea coasts of Egypt, Eritrea, Israel, Jordan, Saudi Arabia, Sudan, and Yemen
Area: 6,300 square miles (16,500 square kilometers)
Fact: More than 260 different species of hard coral have been identified in the central Red Sea.

Legend

■ Coral Reef
☐ Ocean
〰 River
☐ Land

Scale at Equator

Midway Islands, North Pacific

Hawai'ian Islands, Pacific Ocean

Pulley Ridge, Florida

Andros Barrier Reef, Bahamas

NORTH AMERICA

ATLANTIC OCEAN

Mesoamerican Reef, Mexico, Belize, Guatemala, and Honduras

EQUATOR

PACIFIC OCEAN

SOUTH AMERICA

SOUTHERN OCEAN

ARCTIC OCEAN

Raja Ampat Islands

Location: Indonesia
Area: Land and sea area 15,450 square miles (40,000 sq. km)
Fact: Raja Ampat is believed to be the most diverse coral reef ecosystem.

EUROPE

ASIA

Apo Reef, Philippines

Maldives, Indian Ocean

PACIFIC OCEAN

New Caledonia Barrier Reef, South Pacific Ocean

AFRICA

INDIAN OCEAN

Tubbataha Reefs, Sulu Sea

Saya de Malha Banks, Indian Ocean

AUSTRALIA

Great Barrier Reef

Location: Queensland, Australia
Area: 135,000 square miles (350,000 sq. km)
Fact: The Great Barrier Reef is home to more than 1,500 species of fish.

SOUTHERN OCEAN

ANTARCTICA

Coral Reef Climates

Healthy tropical coral reefs grow continuously. Each year, they may grow vertically between 0.39 to 9.8 inches (1 to 25 centimeters) and horizontally up to 1.2 inches (3 cm).

Most tropical coral reefs exist in waters with a temperature range between 61° and 84° Fahrenheit (16° and 29° Celsius). There are few reef-building corals in waters with temperatures below 61°F (16°C).

Tropical reefs must have enough sunlight in order to flourish. Small algae called zooxanthellae live on tropical corals. These algae are what give corals their bright colors. Zooxanthellae need sunlight for **photosynthesis**. This provides the corals with oxygen, since oxygen is one result of photosynthesis. Photosynthesis is only possible down to a depth of around 656 feet (200 m). Beyond this depth, there is not enough light for photosynthesis to take place.

Coral reefs need waves. Waves move the water, which helps carry oxygen, food, and **nutrients** from other parts of the ocean to the corals. Waves also push away debris, such as sand, which might otherwise build up and bury the reef.

Cooler Reefs

Some corals in the Persian Gulf have **adapted** to live in water temperatures that can range from 100°F (38°C) in summer to 55°F (13°C) in winter. Most other corals could not survive such temperature changes.

There are also cold-water corals. These corals are often found in waters with temperatures around 39° to 55°F (4° to 13°C). Cold-water corals may be found just beneath the surface to depths of more than 6,500 feet (1,981 m). In deep water, cold-water corals may receive little to no sunlight. They also lack zooxanthellae algae. To survive in such depths, cold-water corals feed mostly on **plankton**. Cold-water corals are found in every ocean.

Eco Facts

There are two kinds of corals. Hard corals are reef-building corals. They are stiff and look like rocks. Soft corals do not build reefs. Soft corals sway in moving water and often look like plants. Soft corals often grow on reefs formed by hard corals.

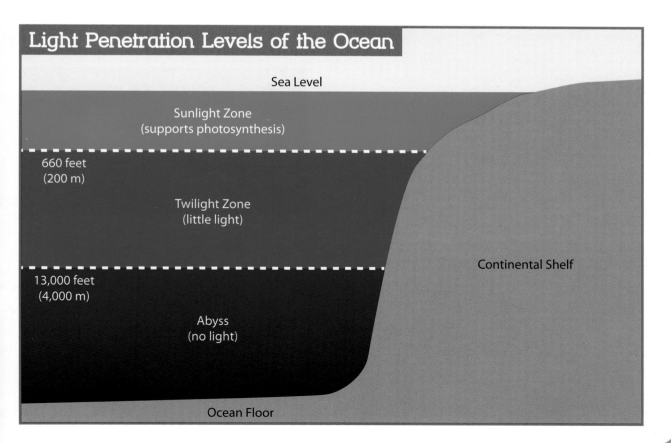

Light Penetration Levels of the Ocean

Sea Level

Sunlight Zone
(supports photosynthesis)

660 feet
(200 m)

Twilight Zone
(little light)

Continental Shelf

13,000 feet
(4,000 m)

Abyss
(no light)

Ocean Floor

Types of Coral Reefs

The type of reef a hard coral forms depends on such things as the depth of the water and the slope of the land. There are three main types of reef that hard corals form. They are fringing reefs, barrier reefs, and atolls.

Fringing Reef

Fringing reefs grow close to land in shallow waters. They can be found on continental shelves along the coastline. Fringing reefs either border the shore beside a shallow channel or **lagoon**, or they are directly attached to the land.

Barrier Reef

Barrier reefs are separated from the shore by a deep channel or lagoon. These reefs can be very large, such as the Great Barrier Reef in Australia. Barrier reefs grow parallel to the coastline but are further out at sea than fringing reefs.

Atolls

Atolls start out as fringing reefs around a volcanic island. When the volcano sinks below the sea, the reef continues to grow. Over time, only the reef remains, close to the surface in a circle around a lagoon. Atolls can take millions of years to form.

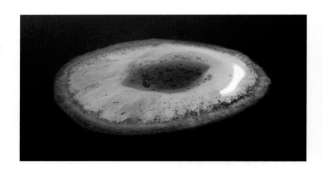

Other Kinds of Reefs

Besides the main three, there are a number of other kinds of reefs. Patch reefs, which are small outcrops of coral, are often located in a lagoon and surrounded by seagrass or sand. There are also bank reefs, apron reefs, ribbon reefs, and table reefs. In the Red Sea, there are reefs called *habili*, which is the Arabic word for "unborn." *Habili* reefs can be a danger to boats because they do not quite break the surface of the ocean.

Features of Coral Reefs

Approximately 800 species of coral are involved in the building of tropical reefs. Coral polyps are very small. They are similar to jellyfish and sea anemones. Though able to live alone, coral polyps most often live in groups and are best-known as part of large reefs.

The reef's main structure is formed by a limestone skeleton called a calicle. The calicle grows at the base of the coral polyp. Once it attaches its calicle to a rock, the polyp divides into thousands of other polyps. The numerous polyps then all connect into a large group, or colony. Over a long period of time, these grow and join other colonies to create reefs.

Mushroom Corals

Not all corals grow in the same way. Mushroom coral polyps grow separately, not in colonies. They can grow up to 10 inches (25 cm) in diameter. Individual colonial coral polyps only grow to about 0.04 to 0.12 inches (1 to 3 millimeters) in diameter. Their colonies can grow to be very large and weigh several tons (tonnes).

Lagoons

Most coral atolls have lagoons. Unlike the reef's rim and the outer reef, which are open to the sea, lagoons are sheltered. Lagoons often contain smaller patch reefs. These can be scattered in small numbers around the lagoon, but in some areas there are large collections of patch reefs. Lagoons vary in depth from just a few feet to more than 230 feet (70 m).

Cays

Cays are low, sandy islands located on the surface of coral reefs. Cays develop when material accumulates in the lagoon or on the reef, forming land above sea level. Plant growth can make the land stable enough to be inhabited and provide space for agricultural and even large residential areas.

Many of the organisms that inhabit coral reefs have adapted to blend in with their environment. This protects them from predators and helps them hunt prey.

Life in Coral Reefs

Coral reefs are some of the most productive ecosystems on Earth. Creatures depend on each other for the food, or energy, they need to survive. This energy transfers between organisms through the food chain.

Producers

The plant-like organisms found on coral reefs are producers. These organisms are called producers because they make their own food. They absorb energy from the Sun and convert it into usable forms of energy, such as sugar. They do this through a process called photosynthesis. Producers found in coral reefs include seagrasses, algae, and plankton.

Primary Consumers

The animals that rely on producers as a food source are called primary consumers. When a primary consumer feeds on a producer, the energy made by the producer is transferred to the consumer. Examples of primary consumers found in coral reef ecosystems include corals, sea turtles, and crabs.

Coral Reef Energy Pyramid

The transfer of energy in an ecosystem begins with producers and moves up the energy pyramid to the tertiary consumers. Organisms at each level of the pyramid receive energy from the organisms in the level below them.

Outside of the pyramid are the decomposers. They break down the dead and decaying **organic** matter left behind when plants and animals die. For this reason, decomposers receive energy from organisms in all levels of the energy pyramid.

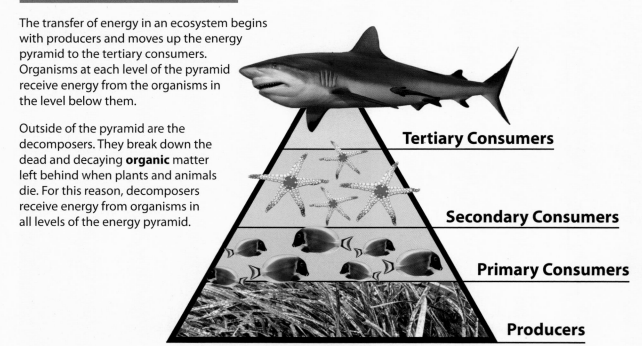

Tertiary Consumers

Secondary Consumers

Primary Consumers

Producers

Coral Reef Food Web

Another way to study the flow of energy through an ecosystem is by examining food chains and food webs. A food chain shows how a producer feeds a primary consumer, which then feeds a secondary consumer, and so on. Most organisms feed on many different food sources. This practice causes food chains to interconnect, creating a food web.

In this example, the **red line** represents one food chain from the plankton to the crab and the shark. The **blue line** from the seagrass to the small fish and to the shark forms another food chain. These food chains connect at the shark, but they also connect in other places. The sea star may feed on the small fish, which may also eat plankton. The crab may feed on seagrass. This series of connections forms a complex food web.

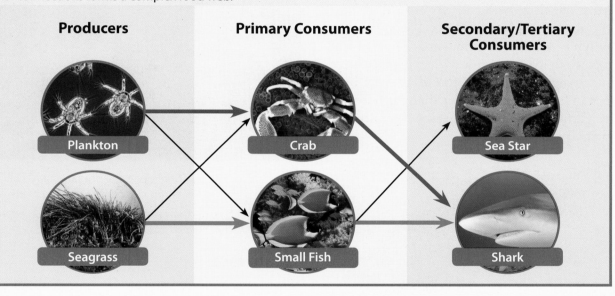

Producers	**Primary Consumers**	**Secondary/Tertiary Consumers**
Plankton	Crab	Sea Star
Seagrass	Small Fish	Shark

Secondary and Tertiary Consumers

Secondary consumers feed on both producers and primary consumers. Around coral reefs, secondary consumers include eels and sea stars. The largest fish, such as sharks and barracuda, are called tertiary consumers. Tertiary consumers feed on both secondary consumers and primary consumers.

Decomposers

Mussels, clams, and many types of bacteria live in coral reef ecosystems. These organisms are called decomposers because they eat dead and decaying organic materials. Some consumers, such as crabs and sea stars, also may be decomposers. Decomposers speed up the process of breaking down organic materials and collect the nutrients to use as energy.

Algae and Plants

Marine algae are small, simple organisms. Many algae create their own food through photosynthesis. Algae, however, are not plants. Seagrasses and mangroves are the plants most commonly associated with coral reefs. Marine algae and plants provide the coral reef with nutrients.

Marine Algae

Marine algae are the only organisms that grow on the part of a reef made up of hard coral. Most of this growth consists of zooxanthellae, the algae that gives corals its colors. The coral polyp is this algae's home, providing it with a place to live and grow. Larger algae, called macroalgae, can also be found on reefs, but not in large quantities. For many species of fish and **invertebrates**, marine algae are the primary food source.

Sunlight is the primary source of energy for coral reef ecosystems.

Seagrasses

Seagrasses require large amounts of sunlight and clear water for the best growth. They are found mostly in temperate and tropical waters. Seagrasses grow in both small patches and huge meadows. They provide a habitat for many organisms, including algae, corals, shrimp, sea turtles, and sea snakes. Many young fish live in seagrasses until they are large enough to survive in the open water.

There are 60 species of seagrass worldwide.

Eco Facts

Seagrasses are very important to the health of coral reefs. In the Great Barrier Reef Marine Park, 13 percent of the seafloor is made up of seagrass, but only 6 percent is made up of coral.

Mangroves

Mangroves are salt-tolerant shoreline plants. They grow in areas with calm waters that only have small waves. Mangroves are not normally found close to the large hard coral structures that make up a reef. When mangroves are present, they are important to the coral reef ecosystem. For example, there are twice as many fish on reefs with mangroves compared to reefs without mangroves. Like seagrasses, mangroves provide nurseries for developing coral reef fish and other marine life.

Some corals may attach themselves to the roots of mangroves.

Fish and Crustaceans

Coral reefs are home to almost 25 percent of the planet's marine life. Besides the colorful coral, reefs are perhaps best-known for the many kinds of fish and other organisms that live in them. There are so many kinds of fish that marine scientists are still finding new species.

Reef Shark

Several shark species live in and around coral reefs. These include the blacktip, Caribbean, and whitetip reef sharks. Most reef sharks are relatively small. The whitetip reef shark, for example, grows to about 5 feet (1.5 m) long.

Reef sharks are among the top **predators** of coral reef ecosystems. Only some larger sharks, such as tiger sharks, will hunt reef sharks. Reef sharks may feed on sea turtles, fish, eels, and crabs. The whitetip reef shark can survive up to six weeks without food.

The Caribbean reef shark can grow up to 10 feet (3 m) long. It is fished for its meat, liver oil, and skin.

Fish

Thousands of fish species live in coral reef ecosystems. Wrasses are a type of fish common in many coral reefs. They are brightly colored, cigar-shaped fish. Most wrasse species are small, but the humphead wrasse can be 8.2 feet (2.5 m) long.

Eels live in cracks and crevices in the reef. They generally feed at night. With their powerful jaws and sharp teeth, they are among the most efficient predators in coral reefs. They eat crabs, octopuses, shrimp, and small fish. Other fish found near coral reefs include angelfish, butterflyfish, pufferfish, scorpionfish, seahorses, and many species of ray. Many of the organisms that live in coral reef systems are venomous.

Lionfish were accidentally introduced to the Caribbean. These predators eat large numbers of fish and are causing a great deal of damage to Caribbean coral reef ecosystems.

Eco Facts

The whale shark is the world's largest fish. It may be found in lagoons and coral atolls, as well as in the open sea. The average adult whale shark is 32 feet (9.8 m) long and can weigh more than 20,000 pounds (9,072 kg).

Crustaceans

Crustaceans are invertebrates. There are more than 50,000 known crustacean species, making crustaceans the most populous group in the world's oceans. Many crustaceans are small, growing to no more than a few inches (cm) long and weighing a few ounces (grams). Some crustaceans, such as crabs and lobsters, are much larger. The largest lobster on record weighed 44 pounds (20 kg).

Crustacean bodies are made up of three parts, the head, the middle or thorax, and the tail. A crustacean has no bones. Instead, it has a hard outer shell called an exoskeleton. An exoskeleton does not grow. As a crustacean grows, it must produce a new exoskeleton beneath the old one. It will then shed the old, smaller exoskeleton. This shedding process is called molting. Crustaceans may molt several times each year.

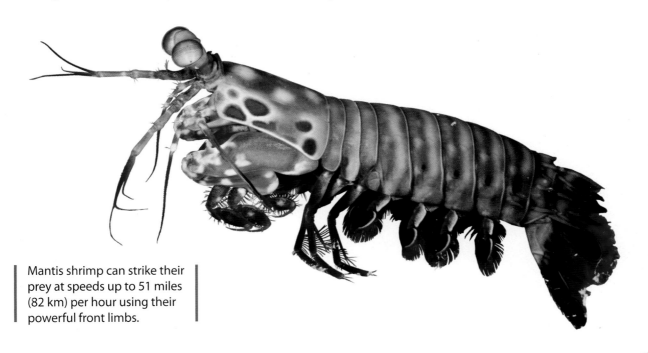

Mantis shrimp can strike their prey at speeds up to 51 miles (82 km) per hour using their powerful front limbs.

Reptiles, Sponges, Echinoderms, and Mollusks

Sea Snakes

Sea snakes live in the waters around reefs in the Indo-Pacific ocean region, except the Red Sea. There are currently more than 60 recognized species. Sea snakes, like land snakes, are air-breathing reptiles. Sea snake bodies are adapted to life in the ocean. To help them swim, sea snakes have paddle-like tails. They feed on fish, eels, **mollusks**, and fish eggs. Sea snakes have small fangs, and many species are extremely venomous. Some species will bite only if provoked, while others are very aggressive. Divers on coral reefs are advised to avoid sea snakes.

The sea snake has large lungs. It can remain underwater for up to 2 hours on a single breath.

Sea Turtles

There are seven species of sea turtles. The species that inhabit coral reefs are the hawksbill turtle, the flatback turtle, and the green sea turtle. Most sea turtles are **carnivores**. Sea turtles range in size from 2 to 6 feet (0.6 to 1.8 m) long. Sea turtles live in both temperate and tropical waters. Most sea turtles are carnivores, but they do not have teeth. Their jaws have adapted to eat certain foods. Some have beaks, some have jaws with serrated edges to tear apart plants. Other species of sea turtle have powerful jaws to crush prey, such as crabs.

Adult green sea turtles only eat plants, such as seagrasses and algae.

Sponges

Several species of these colorful animals may be found on coral reefs. Sponges feed by filtering tiny food particles carried in the water. Sponges are often used as hiding places by crabs, fish, and other small marine creatures. Sponges contain **toxins** that stop most other organisms from trying to eat them.

Echinoderms

Sea cucumbers, sea stars, and sea urchins are **echinoderms** that live in coral reefs. There are more than 1,200 species of sea cucumbers, with most living in the Asia-Pacific region. Sea urchins come in a variety of colors. They move slowly, feeding on algae, and are preyed upon by fish and other marine animals. Sea cucumbers and urchins also contain powerful toxins.

Mollusks

Octopuses, squid, clams, and marine snails live on or near coral reefs. One of the largest reef mollusks is the giant clam. It can grow up to 4 feet (1.2 m) long. Some coral reef mollusks, such as octopuses and some snails, hunt their prey. Other mollusks, such as clams, are filter feeders. They filter plankton and other organic materials directly from the water as it passes by them.

The blue-ringed octopus is one of the most venomous organisms on Earth.

Coral Reefs in Danger

Scientists believe that many of Earth's coral reefs may no longer exist 50 years from now. They also estimate that around 10 percent of the world's reefs may already have been lost forever. Reefs usually survive quite well following natural disasters, but they are less able to deal with damage caused by human activities. Many corals can only survive in very specific water conditions. Any changes to the water quality can upset the balance, threatening to destroy the entire reef.

Agriculture and other industries on land produce runoff that introduces **pesticides**, fertilizers, and other toxic chemicals into the ocean. Sewage is sometimes dumped into the ocean. This is harmful to corals. Land clearing can cause erosion, increasing the level of **sediment** in the water.

Parts of reefs may be chopped away to allow ships and boats into bays and lagoons. Fishing can be a problem for coral reefs, too. Overfishing of one species can upset the balance of the entire ecosystem. In some parts of the world, fishermen use poisons and explosives to catch fish. These can cause great damage to coral reefs. Fishing ships often drag nets, or trawl, along the sea bed to catch fish. This can destroy deepwater corals by ripping them off the reef.

Timeline of Human Activity in Coral Reefs

Australian Aboriginals begin living near the Great Barrier Reef.

Coral, long thought to be a plant, is proposed to be an animal by French naturalist Jean-André Peyssonnel.

British explorer James Cook's ship runs aground on the Great Barrier Reef. It is severely damaged

40,000 BC | **1492 AD** | **1723** | **1768** | **1770** | **1791**

On Christmas Eve, Christopher Columbus' ship, the *Santa Maria*, is wrecked on a coral reef off the coast of what is now Haiti.

French explorer Louis Antoine de Bougainville is the first European to discover the Great Barrier Reef.

HMS Pandora is wrecked on the Great Barrier Reef, killing 35 men.

All ecosystems change and grow over time. If the change occurs too quickly, however, the organisms in that system may not have time to adapt. Scientists believe climate change is raising the temperature of the oceans. They believe this change is happening too quickly for many corals to adapt. An increase in water temperature can cause coral bleaching. This occurs when the water becomes too warm, causing corals to lose the zooxanthellae that live in their tissue and provide them with their colors. An affected coral becomes completely white and, although still alive, more fragile.

Many scientists believe that ocean temperatures will continue to rise in coming years. If this happens, more coral reefs may be lost.

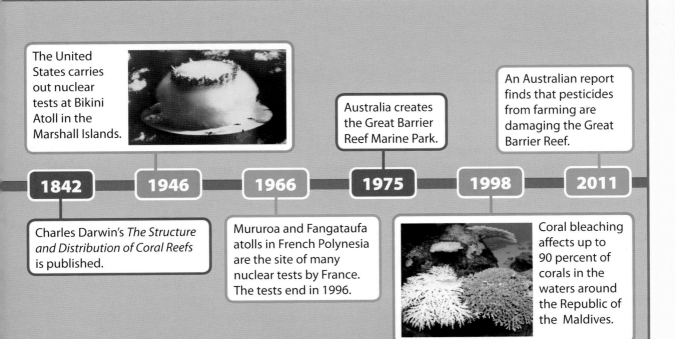

The United States carries out nuclear tests at Bikini Atoll in the Marshall Islands.

Australia creates the Great Barrier Reef Marine Park.

An Australian report finds that pesticides from farming are damaging the Great Barrier Reef.

1842 **1946** **1966** **1975** **1998** **2011**

Charles Darwin's *The Structure and Distribution of Coral Reefs* is published.

Mururoa and Fangataufa atolls in French Polynesia are the site of many nuclear tests by France. The tests end in 1996.

Coral bleaching affects up to 90 percent of corals in the waters around the Republic of the Maldives.

Science in Coral Reefs

Coral reef ecosystems allow scientists to study many organisms in one location.

Coral reefs are diverse ecosystems and scientists study them for different reasons. Some scientists study the organisms and plants that live in the reefs. Others study reefs to see how they might be of use to people. The more scientists study coral reefs, the more they learn just how important coral reefs are.

Coral Reefs and Medicine

Research has shown that coral reef animals and plants may be able to provide important medicines for people. Scientists study coral reef ecosystems to see if the organisms that live in them can be used to develop medicines to treat illnesses, such as Alzheimer's disease, arthritis, bacterial infections, cancer, and heart disease. They also may be of use in the development of new painkillers.

Eco Facts

Coral aquaculture, sometimes called coral farming or coral gardening, is a method of reef conservation. Corals are most at risk of dying in their early growth stage. In aquaculture, coral seeds are grown in nurseries where they can be protected. Later, they are replanted on the reef.

Marine Scientists

Coral reefs can be important indicators of climate change, pollution levels, water quality, and the sustainability of wildlife populations. The development of specialized instruments in recent decades has greatly benefited scientists who study coral reefs. There are instruments for measuring sediment levels, seismometers to measure seafloor movement, and acoustic devices that measure rock and coral formations.

Animal Research

Scientists use radio tagging to learn about animals. Researchers catch animals and attach electronic tags to them, before releasing them into the wild. The tags then broadcast radio signals to research stations, which help track the animals' movements. This can be useful with marine animals, such as some sharks and sea turtles, that may travel throughout the ocean.

Radio tracking helps scientists learn how coral reef habitats are used by organisms. Learning more about the movements of a species can show scientists how to protect endangered animals and environments.

Submarines allow scientists to work in coral reefs for extended periods of time.

Working in Coral Reefs

Many jobs working with coral reefs require a background in biology and chemistry.

From working with wildlife to developing technology and research equipment, there are many exciting and challenging careers related to coral reefs. Before considering these careers, it is important to research the options, learn about the educational requirements, and get hands-on experience with professionals at coastal or marine centers.

Marine Biologist

Duties

Studies coral reef life and how organisms interact with their environment

Education

Bachelor of science, masters, or doctoral degree in marine science

Interests

Biology, ecology, oceanography, the environment

Marine biologists enjoy learning about organisms and their environments. To understand how animals and plants interact with their environments, marine biologists must also study chemical, physical, and geological oceanography. Most marine biologists choose to study a specific subject or species.

Other Coral Reef Jobs

Oceanographer

Studies the physical properties of the ocean, including ocean waves, currents, and geology

Ecologist

Assesses the organisms and habitats in polluted marine ecosystems

Fisheries Officer

Ensures the protection of sensitive coral reef ecosystems by monitoring fishing practices and their effects on the environment

Marine Photographer

Uses photographic equipment to document the ocean and the organisms that inhabit it

Sylvia Earle

Sylvia Earle (born 1935) is an American oceanographer, explorer, marine biologist, lecturer, and author. Among her many accomplishments, Earle is a deep sea explorer-in-residence at the National Geographic Society, leader of the Sustainable Seas Expeditions, and chair of the Advisory Council for the Ocean for Google Earth.

Born in New Jersey, Earle's family moved to Florida when she was 13. Living near the Gulf of Mexico, Earle's love of nature and the outdoors turned toward the sea. After high school, she attended university at Florida State, and went on to earn a doctoral degree in marine biology from Duke University in 1966.

In 1979, Earle set a diving record for women. Her dive to the ocean floor near Oahu in Hawai'i reached a depth of 1,250 feet (381 m). Earle also holds the depth record for a solo dive in a submersible by a woman, at 3,300 feet (1,000 m). In 1982, she and her husband founded Deep Ocean Engineering to develop piloted and robotic underwater devices.

Earle lectures all over the world and has more than 100 published works, including *Exploring the Deep Frontier* and *The Atlas of the Ocean*. She has also written several children's books, such as *Hello Fish* and *Dive!*

Measuring pH Levels

Ocean water is salty and contains many minerals and other substances. It is also slightly acidic. To measure this acidity, scientists measure the **pH balance** of the water. If the acidity level of ocean water changes too much, corals can be damaged and even die.

In this activity, you will make your own paper strips, called pH strips, to test the acidity of different kinds of water. You will need an adult to help.

Materials

Paper coffee filters

Vinegar

Red cabbage

Baking soda

Lemon juice

Water Bottle

1 With the help of an adult, chop the cabbage into small pieces. Boil 1 cup (250 milliliters) of distilled water on the stove. Tap water will not work.

2 Using a blender, have an adult blend the cabbage pieces with just enough tap water to help the cabbage blend well. Dump the blended cabbage into the boiling water. Turn off the heat, and let the water cool.

3 Once cool, use one of the coffee filters to strain the water from the cabbage. Keep the strained water and discard the cabbage. The water should be a deep, red color. You may wish to use rubber gloves so that your hands do not become stained.

4 Soak two coffee filters in the cabbage water thoroughly. Remove the filters and let them dry on something that will not absorb the dye. Once the filters are dry, cut them into strips about 1 inch (2.5 cm) wide. This will give you many pH strips.

5 Make a variety of water mixes, one using the lemon juice, one with vinegar, and one with baking soda. Try different amounts of each substance. Have one that is pure water.

6 Dip a strip into one of the mixtures. Do the same for the other strips and mixtures. The more acidic the water is, the darker red the pH strip will turn. If the water is not acidic, the strip may turn blue or green. The pure water should not change the color of the strip. Ocean water is only slightly acidic.

Create a Food Web

Use this book, and research on the Internet, to create a food web of coral reef ecosystem producers and consumers. Start by finding at least three organisms of each type—producers, primary consumers, secondary consumers, and tertiary consumers. Then, begin linking these organisms together into food chains. Draw the arrows of each food chain in a different color. Use a **red** pen or crayon for one food chain and green and blue for the others. You should find that many of these food chains connect, creating a food web. Add the rest of the arrows to complete the food web using a pencil or **black** pen.

Once your food web is complete, use it to answer the following questions.

1 How would removing one organism from your food web affect the other organisms in the web?

2 What would happen to the rest of the food web if the producers were taken away?

3 How would decomposers fit into the food web?

Sample Food Web

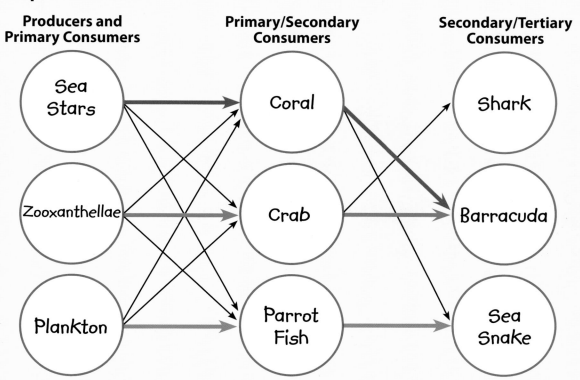

Eco Challenge

1. What are atolls?

2. What is believed to be the most diverse coral reef system?

3. What is the average temperature of the water where most tropical coral reefs are located?

4. What is the world's largest coral reef?

5. How long is the average adult whale shark?

6. How much does a male Aldabra giant tortoise weigh?

7. How long can atolls take to form?

8. How many species of sea cucumbers are there?

9. Where did the United States carry out nuclear tests from 1946 to 1958?

10. What is coral bleaching?

Answers

1. Rings of coral that grow in the ocean on top of inactive, sunken volcanoes
2. Raja Ampat
3. From about 68° to 84°F (20° to 29°C)
4. The Great Barrier Reef
5. 32 feet (9.7 m) long
6. Up to 550 pounds (250 kg)
7. Millions of years
8. More than 1,200
9. Bikini Atoll, Marshall Islands
10. When corals lose the algae providing some of their color and become completely white

Key Words

adapted: changed to suit an environment

carnivores: animals that eat other animals

continental shelf: the edge of a continent

coral polyps: small, tube-shaped animals with mouths that are surrounded by tentacles

echinoderms: invertebrates, usually with five appendages that come out of their bodies

ecosystems: communities of living things sharing an environment

equator: an imaginary line drawn around Earth's center

hemisphere: one half of Earth

invertebrates: animals without backbones

lagoon: a shallow body of water separated from a larger body by reefs or small islands

mollusk: a soft-bodied invertebrate, such as a snail, slug, or octopus

nutrients: substances needed for a healthy life

organic: made up of living things

organisms: living things

pesticides: chemicals used to kill insects

pH balance: the measurement of how acidic a solution is

photosynthesis: the chemical process some plants and algae use to change sunlight into food

plankton: tiny organisms that float in fresh water or seawater

predators: animals that hunt other animals for food

sediment: material that settles at the bottom of a liquid

species: a group of similar organisms that can mate to produce similar offspring

temperate: a climate with mild temperatures

toxins: poisons or venoms

tropical: relating to the warm areas near the equator

Index

Log on to www.av2books.com

AV[2] by Weigl brings you media enhanced books that support active learning. Go to www.av2books.com, and enter the special code found on page 2 of this book. You will gain access to enriched and enhanced content that supplements and complements this book. Content includes video, audio, weblinks, quizzes, a slide show, and activities.

AV[2] Online Navigation

Book Pages
AV[2] pages directly correspond to pages in the book.

Audio
Listen to sections of the book read aloud.

Video
Watch informative video clips.

Embedded Weblinks
Gain additional information for research.

Key Words
Study vocabulary, and complete a matching word activity.

Try This!
Complete activities and hands-on experiments.

Quizzes
Test your knowledge.

Slide Show
View images and captions, and prepare a presentation.

AV[2] was built to bridge the gap between print and digital. We encourage you to tell us what you like and what you want to see in the future.

Sign up to be an AV[2] Ambassador at www.av2books.com/ambassador.